Christmas in New England

Christmas in New England

Photographs by TAYLOR LEWIS, JR.

Text by JOANNE YOUNG

HOLT, RINEHART AND WINSTON
New York   Chicago   San Francisco

ACKNOWLEDGMENTS

This book is the product of many impressions and many people besides ourselves—strangers, old friends, and new ones. Our sincere gratitude goes out to all those who offered us their warm hospitality, their excellent advice, and the benefit of their own experiences to help us in our travels through New England. If we have been able to capture the heart of this warm and happy season, it is in large part due to: David Balfour, Director of Travel, New England Council; Mr. and Mrs. Ernest Pennagio, Newport, R. I.; Miss Margaret Condrick, Boston Chamber of Commerce; Miss Alma Eschenfelder, Mystic Seaport; John Banta and Mrs. Louise Perrin, Historic Deerfield Foundation; Miss Harriet Matson, Rockport, Mass.; Mr. and Mrs. Kenneth Sampson, Brockton, Mass.; Mr. and Mrs. Kenneth Sherman, Providence, R.I.; Mr. and Mrs. Ed Knowlton, Charlton City, Mass.; James Venetos, Deerfield Inn, Deerfield, Mass.; Richard Brams, The Publick House, Sturbridge, Mass., Francis Kopeis, The Wayside Inn, South Sudbury, Mass.; Mr. and Mrs. Herman Erwin, Peg Leg Inn, Rockport, Mass.; Mr. and Mrs. Rene Chardin and family, Four Columns Inn, Newfane, Vt.; Enoch Fuller, Fitzwilliam Inn, Fitzwilliam, N.H.; Alfred Sawyer, Silver Ranch, Jaffrey, N.H.; Parker Whitcomb, East Hill Farm, Troy, N.H.; Ray Harney, Revere, Mass.; Dr. Harold S. Burr, Old Lyme, Conn.; Dr. Leonard J. Ravitz, Norfolk, Va.; Miss Katharine Lyford, Boston, Mass.; and dozens of other New Englanders who shared their own Christmas spirit with us. And our special gratitude to Bob, Nancy, Randy, and Mark Young, and Polly, Taylor B., Kimberly, Sam, and Troy Lewis with whom we kept Christmas in our hearts.

Locations for photographs not otherwise identified are: Stowe, Vt., pp. 6, 7; Silver Ranch, Jaffrey, N.H., p. 10; Townshend, Vt., p. 11, top; Newfane, Vt., pp. 11, bottom, 18, 19; near Newfane, Vt., p. 12; Longfellow's Wayside Inn, South Sudbury, Mass., pp. 13, 16; Temple Mountain, N.H., pp. 14, 15; near Orleans, Cape Cod, p. 17; Peg Leg Inn, Rockport, Mass., p. 25; Rockport, Mass., pp. 27, 29; Filene's and Boston Market, pp. 42, 43; Greenman house, Mystic Seaport, p. 44; Ipswich, Mass., p. 45; Wayne Morrell Gallery, Rockport, Mass., p. 47; First Baptist Meeting House from the Providence (R.I.) Art Club, p. 48; Deerfield (Mass.) Inn, p. 49; the Rene Chardin family and guests, Four Columns Inn, Newfane, Vt., pp. 58, 59; Louisburg Square, Boston, p. 61; Congregational Church, Rockport, Mass., p. 62; King's Chapel, Boston, p. 63, top; South Walden Methodist Church, Vt., p. 63, bottom; Bear Skin Neck, Rockport, Mass., p. 64.

Published simultaneously in Canada by Holt, Rinehart and Winston of Canada, Limited.

Library of Congress Catalog Card Number: 72–78103

ISBN: 0–03–091992–4

First Edition

Designer: WILLIAM LANYON

Printed in the United States of America

The weather vane on top of the red barn—the white church—the shingled house—swings on its axis and blows to the north. Large lazy flakes of snow begin to sift gently from a sky that has turned from blue to gray since morning and cling, almost lovingly, to the trees. Soon the snow begins to drift in New England woods where maples still wear golden-brown leaves among silver birches and green pines.

*B*arns have been made snug for the winter; full silos look as though they, like the cattle, have huddled closer together for warmth. Blue haze hangs over the mountains. On some days the valleys fill up with fog, or low-hanging clouds settle down in the notches.

When winter storms threaten, New England farms are like small, sturdy fortresses, drawing in the family, the dog, the cat, to their snug hearthsides. Tall woodpiles, which have grown daily next to barns or back doors, promise that fires will stay kindled. A full pantry and freezer, where the summer's largesse has been stored, assure that even a growing boy's endless appetite will be satisfied, no matter how high the snow drifts rise between the house and road.

Besides, who worries about the weather when the calendar shows that each crossed-out day is bringing you closer to Christmas, and every closet holds a secret? If the radio says, "Heavy snow warnings are up; no school today," there are surprises to plan, packages to wrap and hide, and a whole basket of chestnuts to roast over the fire.

Even more interesting is the spicy aroma escaping from the kitchen—a medley of fruits and nuts, sweet batter, and a heady suggestion of rum or brandy that can only mean the mouth-watering ritual of baking fruit cakes has begun. There are bowls to lick, pecans and walnuts to shell, and best of all, a bite of the little "test cake" to taste before the rest are put away to age properly till Christmas.

Stocking-capped boys and girls from Canaan, Connecticut, to Calais, Maine, are dusting off their sleds and sharpening their ice skates. Smaller youngsters carefully write their letters to Santa Claus ("I have been very good this year!") and by the fire old men reminisce of boyhood Christmases.

"Those were cold winters," recalls Dr. Harold S. Burr, puffing on his cigar. "When I was a boy, this house was heated by a big wood stove downstairs. At night we lit the oil lamps—candles, too. My grandfather owned the house then—he was a Calvinist minister. About all he let us do to celebrate Christmas was go to church. In fact, we went to church on the slightest excuse all week and three or four times on Sunday!"

Dr. Burr's companion, Howell Maynard, rocks thoughtfully and gazes a

A log fire and a friendly mug at Mansewood near Old Lyme, Connecticut, home of the Burr family since it was built about 1730

After a long, exhilarating day on wilderness trails covered with new snow, a tired skier heads for his remote lodge in Vermont's Mount Snow area.

At far left, a farm nestles in the valley near Waterbury Center, Vermont, the blue hills standing guard beyond the winter woods.

long way into the fire. He, too, knew Connecticut at Christmas as a boy.

"Eh-yup, we had worse winters then. Sometimes took ten yoke of oxen to plow out the road after a big snow. Many's the time I walked to school on top of the stone fence before the road was plowed. Week before Christmas, we'd cut a little tree on our farm and hang paper chains and strings of cranberries and popcorn balls on it. Christmas morning, we'd each open one or two little presents from our folks, and we'd take the sleigh to church. It was simpler then, but we enjoyed it more."

Dr. Burr agreed. "We made our own toys—I made skis out of barrel staves, and they worked real well."

"Christmas dinner was a real feast," Mr. Maynard remembered. "Mother and the girls set a long table the whole length of the kitchen. Sometimes we had chickens, or duck—sometimes only spare ribs, but they were real tasty! Then there were potatoes and vegetables and cranberries and pies." His eyes warmed at the memory, and the fire crackled quietly on the hearth. . . .

Sleigh bells jingle merrily in the winter stillness—the one-horse-open-sleigh no longer a necessity but still a well-loved part of New England holidays. The gentle clop of the horse's hoofs is muted in the snow, but startled crows and blue jays noisily announce the sleigh's passage across the snow.

General stores in every town and crossroad lay in their winter supply of rock salt and snow shovels, toboggans, ski wax, and—of course—wreaths and lights and tinsel and Christmas tree balls!

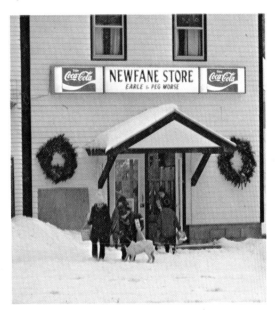

11

At the First Church of Deerfield in Old Deerfield, Massachusetts—and at countless other churches and grange halls throughout New England—plans for a Christmas "giving" are under way. The lovely, old, brick church sits halfway down The Street which is lined with elms planted more than a century and a half ago by the Reverend Samuel Willard when he was its preacher. Today the minister is meeting with a county welfare worker to discuss which families may not be able to have a merry Christmas without help. In the minister's study, they discuss whose crops were bad this year, whose budget was overwhelmed by accident or illness. Word of the most appropriate gifts is quietly passed around, but the names are carefully guarded, for New Englanders respect the spirit of proud independence which they and their neighbors share. On the Sunday before Christmas, following the custom of many years, the congregation will arrive with their white-wrapped gifts and place them under the tree in a corner of the sanctuary. On Christmas Eve, they are delivered.

Before the three schools let out for the winter holiday, a crèche is placed on the common, and the Bement School students and faculty walk the mile-long street to sing wherever they see a shining candle in an ancient window.

At the Wapping School House, where the fragrance of spiced tea brewing mingles with the scent of pine, the staff of the Heritage Foundation are at work making Christmas wreaths for the doors of historic buildings. Simplicity must be the keynote so as not to detract from the doors themselves, each one an architectural treasure with its bullet glass or its delicate fanlight. Christmas music is playing as the ladies' skillful fingers wire pine cones and holly berries and bright red ribbons in place. In this serene little town where the past is preserved and treasured, Christmas is on its way.

Each slope has its own attraction—the gentler trails beckoning novices; the steep mountain faces, the breath-taking jumps challenging the experts. For others, cross-country trails with their scenic vistas of glittering hills and sunlit valleys are the lure. But for everyone, *après ski* holds the charm

Perhaps no one in New England loves Christmas more than the ski enthusiasts. At least it's easy to get that impression, for in ski lodges throughout the White Mountains, the Green Mountains, and the Berkshire Hills, Christmas decorations stay up until Easter! The Christmas season is by far the most popular time for a ski vacation, and long before the first snow flurry, skiers book their reservations at their favorite inn or winter resort. Then comes the season of sky-watching when every skier and resort owner listens tensely for weather reports and scans the horizon for those gray snow clouds.

at day's end—a fire to warm your hands, friends to warm your heart, and the cup that cheers to dispel the chill of wind and weather. At many resorts, an Alpine atmosphere extends indoors from the mountain ranges. In a decor distinctly Swiss or Bavarian, skiers gather around bubbling fondue pots where a loaf of crusty bread and a bottle of good wine complete the cuisine. At other resorts, the venerable New England inns which have offered their warm hospitality to wayfarers since Colonial days provide it equally to twentieth-century holiday visitors, who ski on nearby slopes.

In 1604, on a tiny island off the coast of Maine, the first recorded celebration of Christmas in New England was held. Here at St. Croix (now called Dochet Island), a group of eighty French settlers, among them Father Nichols d'Aubri and a Huguenot minister, held Christmas services in their rough, timber chapel. Then, with as much merriment as they could muster in this rugged climate, so different from that of their native land, they held traditional sporting events as they had

done on *le jour de Noël* in France.

The Pilgrim fathers who arrived at Cape Cod sixteen years later permitted no such frivolity! Christmas, they declared, was a human invention since Christ's birth date was unknown; and because it coincided with pagan celebrations of the Winter Solstice, its observance by Christians was a "corruption." So carefully did they *not* acknowledge it that their governor, William Bradford, recorded that at Plymouth, Massachusetts, on "the 25th

day [of December they] began to erect the first house for common use. . . ."

Not all settlers who arrived on the *Mayflower* were Puritans, and the following year (1621) Bradford's history notes: "On the day called Christmas Day, the Governor called them out to work. . . . But the most of this company excused themselves and said it went against their consciences to work on that day. So the Governor told them that if they made it a matter of conscience, he would spare them till they were better informed; so he led away the rest and left them. But when they came home at noon from their work, he found them in the street at play, openly; some pitching the bar, and some at stool-ball and such like sports. So he went to them and took away their implements, and told them that was against his conscience, that they should play and others work. If they made it a matter of devotion, let them keep [to] their houses, but there should be no gaming or revelry in the streets."

Drive into a little New England town in mid-December, and you have the feeling that you have been magically transported into a Currier and Ives etching, or at least a Christmas card! No matter whether it is Newfane, Vermont; Fitzwilliam, New Hampshire; Wiscasset, Maine; Litchfield, Connecticut; or Concord, Massachusetts—here is the snow-covered green in the heart of town, bordered by a white church with its delicate spire, stately Colonial houses, the inn, the library, and the town hall. Here on the green is the memorial to a Civil War soldier, and nearby the community Christmas tree and a lighted crèche. Footsteps and traffic sounds are snow-muffled, but the bell which peals the

hour has the sound of ringing crystal in the clear, winter air. Wisps of woodsmoke curl from chimney tops, and the church door wears its handsome wreath of evergreens tied with a large red bow. Here is the ice-covered pond where children are skating, the red barn, the icicles on the eaves, and beyond all the encircling hills. It has changed very little since the turn of the century, at least on the surface. Numbers by front doors often appear to be street addresses—1748, 1769, 1750, then a jump to 1830. However, these are not for the postman, but a record of when the houses were built. At the country store, housewives arrive early (the young ones often pulling a sled on which sits a baby, completely bundled up except for his rosy, button

nose!). They are most often bound for the grocery section that is well-stocked with all the ingredients for cookie baking which will keep kitchens fragrant and youngsters' mouths watering for weeks. When the school bus returns in mid-afternoon, there is another flurry of activity, usually centered around the candy counter.

In medium-sized towns, street decorations go up, usually put in place by intrepid volunteers from the top of a fire engine ladder. The tinsel, the lights, the bells, and stars are always gay and often gaudy, giving the streets a festive air. In Rockport, Massachusetts, they are particularly beautiful—small green Christmas trees, twinkling with colored lights, high on poles that line Main Street and Bearskin Neck. Since before the Civil War, this picturesque little town which hugs the rocky coast of Cape Ann has been a favorite with artists. They have set up their easels along the narrow village streets, the weathered fishing wharves, or the smooth half-moon of sandy beach. Many have stayed and made it their home.

Trimming a town is harder than trimming a tree, this fireman discovers in Littleton, New Hampshire.

Youngsters on Christmas vacation play hockey in Gloucester, Massachusetts.

At far right, a penny still buys a sweet satisfying stick of candy at The Village Traders' country store in Newfane, Vermont.

At Christmas each year, the artists return a gift of beauty to Rockport, a pageant which moves from the tip of Bearskin Neck, lined with the artists' colorful shops whose frosty, lighted windows hold their wares like jewels, to the crèche on the lawn of the First Congregational Church at the top of the hill. On the Sunday afternoon before Christmas, the historic Old Tavern, home of the Rockport Art Association, is a beehive of activity as a cast of nearly one hundred arrives to don their costumes. Roles are often handed down from father to son, and one small shepherd boy was heard to tell another, "Someday I'm going to be one of the Three Wise Guys!" By dusk, Rockport's streets are lined with visitors as the first glowing torches appear at the head of a band of Roman soldiers. The carols fade, and a resonant voice at the microphone begins to read, "And it came to pass in those days that there

went out a decree from Caesar Augustus that all the world should be taxed."

Snow is falling gently, and it adds to the hush that falls over the crowd as the pageant proceeds up the hill. Here comes the little caravan from Naz-

areth, the gentle donkey with Mary, his precious burden; Joseph with his staff; others on their way to Bethlehem, one group leading a cow. They stop at the Inn built on the lawn in front of the Art Association, but the innkeeper tells them there is no room, and they move on up the road to the stable. "And so it was that while they were there, the days were accomplished that she should be delivered, and she brought forth her first-born son, and wrapped him in swaddling clothes, and laid him in a manger."

The Congregational choir bursts into song, and one by one the torchlit group of shepherds, an excited group of costumed children, and the majestic wise men make their way up the snowy hill to present their gifts.

Suddenly it is over; the costumed artists and their families move out to the streets, the crowd follows, and a guitarist at the head of the march begins to strum "Oh, Come All Ye Faithful."

Left, this foursquare old captain's house is framed by ancient trees as dusk falls in Yarmouth, Maine.

In the Clock Shop on Main Street in Ipswich, Massachusetts, the clocks tick merrily toward Christmas.

The cock on the weather vane seems to be crowing the good news to the surrounding countryside.

The whole town, it seems, is caroling! Through the snow they walk, singing the happy songs of Christmas, and the happy spirit of it fills the night. . . .

It is hard to believe that just a gull's flight from Cape Ann, at Marblehead and Ipswich and Salem when Puritanism was at its height, the term "Christmas Keeper" was a dangerous accusation! The General Court of Massachusetts in 1659 enacted a law which read, "Whosoever shall be found observing any such days as Christmas or the like, either by forebearance of labor or feasting, or in any other way as a festival shall be fined five shillings!" To make it still more specific, and to include in the prohibition even cooks and certain musicians, the Puritans spelled it out: "No one shall read

Common Prayer, keep Christmas or saints' days, make minced pie, dance, play cards, or play on any instrument of music except the drum, trumpet, and jews-harp." But it's hard to keep high spirits down, particularly among Yankees, and gradually the Christmas Keepers won small concessions, such as being allowed to exhibit a polar bear on Boston Common.

Actually, it was not until the mid-nineteenth century that the celebration of Christmas was accepted generally outside the Episcopal, Roman Catholic, or Unitarian churches in New England. Where immigrants from Germany, Portugal, or Ireland arrived along with the Industrial Revolution, they brought the customs of their homelands which gradually mingled with those of less rigid English denominations. When the Christmas season at last became a New England holiday, it had absorbed many of the most endearing and enduring traditions of many countries—like America herself. It included the German Christmas tree, the Dutch Saint Nicholas, the evergreen and mistletoe decorations of the Scandinavians, the beloved carols of all these people, and holiday foods that had a flavor of the best of many mother countries along with dishes unique to New England woods and waters.

The roast beef of old England is still a New England specialty at the White Horse Tavern, Newport, Rhode Island.

Gadsby the Goose is a Christmas tradition with the John P. Evrards of Providence, Rhode Island.

When the Pilgrims and their friends, the Wampanoag Indians under Chief Massasoit, held the first Thanksgiving in 1621, Edward Winslow wrote an English friend that their feast included wild turkeys and venison, which not surprisingly, later took a place on the Christmas table. Add roast goose or duck, chestnut dressing, cranberries that abound in the tidelands, wild rice, succulent oysters—at their best in December—and other shellfish delicacies which the New England coast provides in abundance, and you have a gourmet's dream. Block Islanders have their own specialty, known with tongue in cheek as Block Island turkey, which is, in fact, the venerable codfish, baked to perfection in Rhode Island fashion, its stuffing fragrant with herbs and onions.

The butcher wraps up a Christmas turkey in the Newfane (Vermont) Store.

A festive roast goose at The Wayside Inn, South Sudbury, Massachusetts.

On Christmas Eve, Nauset Light stands guard on Cape Cod, her great eye sweeping majestically over the dark water as on every other night of the year. All along the 6,000 miles of New England coast, lighthouses send out their beams from dusk to dawn to guide a lobsterboat with a tiny Christmas tree on its wooden mast or a sleek Navy ship racing home for the holidays at Newport. The lighthouses are still as unfailing a beacon in fog or storm as they were to a China clipper bound out of Salem 200 years ago. Their keepers are in the staunch tradition of surfmen who, until a few years ago, patroled the beaches from each light station seven miles to the "halfway house" and back again, three times each night in winter. Henry Beston, one of the most sensitive chroniclers of life on the Cape, described in *The Outermost House* such a winter night in 1928 when less isolated New Englanders were trimming their Christmas trees, forgetful of the weather. "The snow skirred along the beach, the wind suffering it no rest; I saw little whirlpools of it driving down the sand into the onrush of the breakers; it gathered in the footprints of the coast guard patrols, building up their leeward side and patterning them in white on the empty beach. The snow in the air had a character of its own for it was the snow of the outer Cape and the North Atlantic, snow icy and crystalline, and sweeping across the dunes and moors rather than down upon them. Chancing to look to the north, I saw Nauset Light still turning and gleaming. . . ." Such is Christmas on Cape Cod, with a lonelier, more elemental beauty than Boston's, but merry in its own way. A wreath as cheerful as any on Beacon Hill hangs on the Nauset Light station door; and as the light above suddenly breaks through the cold sunset dusk on the cliff, the twinkling lights of a Christmas tree can be seen through the window. They say, as clearly and subtly as though the words were spoken in the inimitable New England accent, that Christmas is a thing of the heart, after all, with its own warmth to offset the winter winds and drifting snow.

Two seafaring men, carved in the style of figureheads, flank a shop door at Boothbay Harbor, Maine.

The houses of Gloucester, Massachusetts, turn their faces seaward as their men have turned fishing boats for generations.

On Christmas morning the sun breaks first in the United States at West Quoddy Head, the easternmost point on the shore of Maine. Farther down the coast, where hundreds of rocky fingers of land extend into the Atlantic, lies Christmas Cove. Captain John Smith, exploring out of Jamestown, sailed into this little harbor where pine, spruce, and oak grow down to the icy water's edge, on Christmas Day in 1614. He established fisheries on nearby Monhegan Island, one of the earliest sites of New England's fishing industry. So much of New England life is bound up in her seafarers that it is impossible to separate the two. Wood-carvers who created the colorful figureheads for sailing vessels (many seamen refused to sail on a ship without one) turned their skillful hands at slack season to allied arts. They carved intricate ships' models, or elaborate decorations for houses—fluted columns, reeded pilasters, classical urns for fence posts. New England's great shipbuilding towns —Salem, East Boston, and Bath and Kittery, Maine—abound with examples.

Lobster pots of the wharf
and gently rocking dories
are frosted with snow at
Rockport, Massachusetts.

Even the sun looks cold at
Boothbay Harbor, Maine,
where only a few fishing
boats ventured out this
early December morning.

Facing page, top, brightly
painted floats on a Maine
lobsterman's shack look
almost like a new kind of
Christmas tree ornament.

Along with wood carving, another unique art grew among sailing men. Whalers with time on their hands as they waited for the cry "Thar she blows!" began etching on whalebone and carving delicate little objects out of whale teeth. These became known as scrimshaw, and doubtless many a tiny figurine or etched scene of a foreign port became a Christmas gift for a Nantucket wife or sweetheart after a long voyage. And what other exotic gifts were found under New England Christmas trees after the China trade opened and Yankee clippers seemingly flew back and forth around Cape Horn? Tea and spices, certainly, but also beautiful silk fabrics, inlaid fans, jewelry and even furniture in the Oriental style. The homes of ship's captains were indeed cosmopolitan in decor. With the dawn of the Steam Age in the late nineteenth century, some of the romance went out of the sea. The assurance that it will

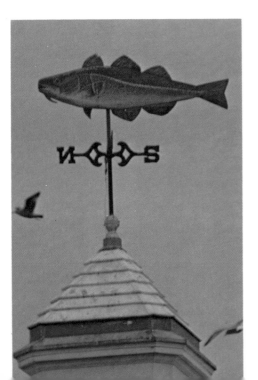

never disappear entirely is partly the result of a meeting held on Christmas Day in 1929 when the Marine Historical Association was formed at Mystic, Connecticut. Where a shipyard thrived a century ago now stands a living maritime museum from which great ships still sail and where others are permanently docked. The wooden whaleship, *Charles W. Morgan,* lies at anchor here, and nearby are the fishing schooner, *L. A. Dunton* and many others. Along the cobbled streets still stand the typical buildings of a fishing village.

At Mystic Seaport on the Sunday before Christmas, the Seaport Carolers stroll through the streets, leading thousands of visitors in a carol sing. Floodlights play on the rigging of the old ships and the Christmas trees on top of the masts, and a community tree in front of the Aloha Meeting House glistens with lights. In the parlor of the Greenman house, a marvelous Victorian tree nearly fills the room; and at the children's museum is a delightfully whimsical tree, decorated entirely with sea shells of all shapes and sizes.

On Cape Cod, a primitive weathervane points windward near North Truro.

The fruits of the sea make a sumptuous holiday feast at the White Horse Tavern in Newport, Rhode Island —lobster taking place of honor with clams and shrimp.

At Christmas time, the lights of Mystic Seaport reflect on the river, and the romance of sailing days comes alive again.

There are those who feel that Boston is the hub of the universe. It is, at least, the heart of New England at Christmas or any other time of year! The sun has set by four o'clock on a winter day, and the hundreds of lights on the city's fabulous department stores sparkle brilliantly on the shoppers below who rush madly on last-minute errands. Bells in the church towers around Boston Common toll the hours till Christmas in merry voices. Feet hurt, and packages are jostled; cab drivers weave in and out of traffic precariously, while waiters who thought they'd never make it through the noon rush hour try to catch a breath before the dinner crowd

arrives. Clerks wait on three customers at once, at least one of whom cannot remember what Aunt Minnie said she wanted or what size shirt Cousin Bill wears! In short, it is Christmas chaos—which would be unbearable at any other time of year, but which just now is magically underscored with patience and good humor. At Jordan Marsh's Enchanted Village, the delight of children watching the almost life-size puppets in storybook houses is contagious. The children twitter like little birds: "Lookit! There's a bakery!" "Lookit! That boy's mixing a cake." "That chicken's laying an egg!" "It's a candy shop—lookit the lollipops." "Lookit the cat on the roof!"

A gray-haired lady in a venerable tweed coat touches your arm and nods at a long-haired, teen-age couple who are gazing arm in arm at the farm scene. "Lookit them—aren't they sweet?" she says. Lookit—lookit—while little blue and brown and black eyes shine like Christmas stars. Lookit and enjoy your own childhood all over again. . . .

The Boston Market is another scene out of Christmases past and present— joyful, colorful, and constantly in motion. In the shadow of Faneuil Hall, where Samuel Adams once exhorted the fiery Sons of Liberty, the market continues to operate much as it did in Colonial days. At Christmas it is a seething scene of bargaining and ex-

changing of goods and money as aristo-crats in tailor-made suits vie with blue-jeaned couples for Christmas trees, mistletoe, pine wreaths, garlands, and poinsettias. For a moment, the scent of pine woods invades the heart of Boston, and one after another customer leaves with the best-looking tree on the lot on his shoulder while another truckload arrives from Christmas tree farms tucked into the Bay State's hills.

Every large store has its own Santa Claus, with long lines of eager children waiting to confide their Christmas dreams. The State of Massachusetts has its own official Santa whose license plate reads: SANTA C. His days are filled at this season with visits to orphanages and old people's homes to distribute his goodies from a bulging pack.

New Englanders may be especially fond of the jolly saint because Clement Clark Moore, who popularized him for American children in 1823 ("Twas the night before Christmas, and all through the house . . ."), resided for a time in Newport, Rhode Island. Professor Moore undoubtedly drew on the description by Washington Irving, a New York neighbor, whose *Knickerbocker's History of New York* related Saint Nick's visit to the Dutch settlers: ". . . and lo! the good St. Nicholas came riding over the tops of the trees, in that self-same wagon wherein he brings his yearly presents to children. . . . And the shrewd Van Kortlandt knew him by his broad hat, [and] his long pipe. . . . And he lighted his pipe by the fire and sat himself down and smoked. . . . And when St. Nicholas had smoked his pipe, he twisted it in his hat-band, and laying his finger beside his nose, gave the astonished Van Kortlandt a

very significant wink; then, mounting his wagon, he returned over the tree-tops and disappeared. . . ."

The birth date of Christmas customs is hard to pinpoint because only in retrospect does each seem important enough to record. Among the first Christmas trees in New England was one decorated by John Bushmann in Westfield, Massachusetts, in 1860 following the custom of his childhood in Germany.

By the Victorian era, visions of sugar plums danced in the heads of hundreds of little boys in velvet suits and patent leather pumps and beribboned girls with muffs and plumed hats—or so it seems from the newspaper ads and illustrations of that day. In 1870, Marcus Ward & Co. of London introduced Christmas cards to New England importers, and a few years later, L. Prang & Co. of Boston began to compete with its own line. In 1880 and 1881, Prang offered a prize for the best original designs, and 600 were submitted! Some breathed sentiment in every line:

I caught her as she flitted past,
  I whispered "I have you now!"
I caught her and I held her fast,
  Under the mistletoe-bough!

A touch of dainty finger-tips,
And then, I hardly know how,
I kissed her cheek, I kissed her
lips
Under the mistletoe-bough!

In 1921, Boston instituted a tradition which continues to this day. A community Christmas tree was set up on snowy Boston Common, and the choirs of the city were invited to gather around it and present a concert of carols. With the elegant town houses of Charles Street in the background, and ice skaters gliding by on the pond, Boston Common still looks remarkably like a Victorian Christmas card! Other New England cities now have community celebrations, among them Hartford, Connecticut, with its breath-taking Festival of Lights; and Newport, Rhode Island, where Atlantic Fleet ships at the U. S. Naval Base are lit up from stem to stern like a Christmas tree.

Along the steep, often cobbled streets of the historic College Hill area of Providence, Rhode Island, the Christmas season looks at home. The simple doorways of colorful Benefit Street houses seem designed for the handsome wreaths that adorn them, and snow decorates the trees along the

curbstones. In most of New England, wherever a holiday table is set—from a beautiful Colonial dining room with candles gleaming on polished silver to a simple farmhouse deep in the hills— restraint seems to be a part of the regional architecture of all periods. Old houses are loved, artfully restored, and their style suits the rugged character of the land and its people.

The snow-capped lantern of the Providence Art Club; beyond, the delicate spire of the First Baptist Meeting House.

To drive along Narragansett Bay and turn onto the famous "ten mile drive" on Newport's rugged coastline is, seemingly, to enter another country. A few hundred yards beyond weathered wharves where fishing boats are docked sit Tudor castles, French chateaux, and Renaissance palazzi—Miramar, Belcourt Castle, Rosecliff, The Breakers, Eagle's Nest. To add to the mental confusion, these opulent palaces, garlanded for Christmas like duchesses wearing diamond necklaces around their plump throats, are called "summer cottages"! These are the fabulous mansions that millionaires with a longing for European grandeur built in the pre-income tax days at the turn of the century. Marble House, the summer home of the William K. Vanderbilts, which was designed by architect Rich-

Left, Marble House in Newport, Rhode Island.

Below, the parlor at The Wayside Inn, South Sudbury, Massachusetts.

ard Morris Hunt of Brattleboro, Vermont, is open to visitors at Christmas. The mansion glitters inside and out as it did in the era when perfumed ladies swept down its marble staircase to dance in its magnificent ballroom with white-tied gentlemen. The carriage lights around the circular driveway glow in the dusk as though at any moment a liveried chauffeur at the wheel of one of those daring new motorcars (a Pierce Arrow perhaps?) might pull up to the portico. The marble fountain in the entry hall, its water forever frozen in glistening silver, is heaped with poinsettia, pine, and spruce and twinkling with tiny lights. The arched windows overlooking the ocean at Cliff Walk wear Christmas wreaths of baronial scale to match the room; soft light flickers from the crystal chandelier. It is a fairytale house from a fairytale age.

On December 23, the Armory of the Artillery Company of Newport, on Thames Street, is the scene of unusual

A glazed ham is a delight to both eye and palate at The Publick House in Sturbridge, Massachusetts.

activity. Most of the year, tourists interested in the Armory's fascinating memorabilia on military history flock to its doors, but tonight something much more festive is under way. Shiny black limousines from the nearby U. S. Naval War College and the Naval Base pull up along the narrow street, and beribboned officers in dress uniforms step out. In between, low-slung sports cars or station wagons appear, from whose depths other officers alight, but these men are in the white knee breeches, the bright blue and red coats of the Colonial militia! All of them disappear jovially inside the huge bewreathed doors under the watchful eye of a carved golden eagle that once reposed on the paddle-wheel box of the New York steamer *Metropolis*. This distinguished, if unusual, assemblage is celebrating not only Christmas but Saint Barbara's Day— Saint Barbara being the patroness of artillery. All seem magnetically drawn to a huge and splendid silver punch bowl, the pride of the Company. The bowl itself is fashioned from a very special metal—the melted-down rank and proficiency badges of Army officers who attended the War College between 1967 and the Army's birthday in June, 1971, when the bowl was presented to the Company.

The dining room is decked with holly and Christmas greenery at Deerfield Inn, Deerfield, Massachusetts.

The bowl's contents are equally unusual—a historic Artillery Punch whose secret recipe, made by artillerymen around the world for generations, includes these ingredients in carefully guarded quantities: brandy, gin, bourbon, wines, fruit juices, and sugar. Most important of all, in the bottom of the bowl is placed a mule shoe, from an artillery mule, of course. The concoction is then stirred with a bayonet before serving. The mule shoe is respectfully kept from year to year, and just before the punch-making ceremony the shoe is held in a roaring fire and then quenched in olive oil for purification. It is hard to say if it was from this punch that the saying arose that a drink "had the kick of a mule"—but it is not impossible.

The origin of the Artillery Company celebration goes back to 1780 when French forces under Rochambeau arrived and were quartered in Newport as the British retreated. The French were highly honored guests, particularly after the previous winter when British occupation forces so depleted the city's firewood that the residents were forced to draw lots after the British left to determine which of Newport's houses would be demolished each week for fuel! Consequently, when the citizens realized that these French allies were an ocean away from their families and no doubt homesick at the Christmas season, they decided to entertain the Frenchmen with a gala holiday celebration. The Artillery Company of Newport, which had been formed as a branch of the Rhode Island militia in 1741, took the lead. They marched from the Armory in full regalia (some still in Royal uniforms since Colonial ones were in short supply) down the icy, cobbled streets to the old Colony House where the French met them. Among the guests were the Comte de Rochambeau, the Comte de Grasse, the Admiral de Ternay, and a legendary member of the Swedish Guards serving with the French Army, Alex de Fersen, said to be a lover of Marie Antoinette. A Newport church choir sang Christmas carols, and—although the fact is not recorded—along with wishes for a *Joyeux Noël* in Rhode Island accents, perhaps the Newporters toasted the Frenchmen's health in Artillery Punch.

Artillery punch is the order of the day at the Armory of the Artillery Company of Newport whose men have served in every major conflict since the French and Indian War.

In case they don't have a mule shoe to flavor their Christmas beverages, New Englanders can fall back on an equally traditional drink that guarantees to ward off the effect of winter chill with a warm glow. Hot buttered rum—fragrant with cloves and cinnamon, with a pat of butter melting on the top—is so delicious a winter drink that it may well have inspired the West Indies rum trade in the days of clipper ships. It is only one of the festive ingredients which make the annual Boar's Head feast and Yule Log procession at The Publick House in Sturbridge, Massachusetts, a highlight for holiday travelers. All

the traditions of an old English yule are carried on in this famous old inn, built by Colonel Ebenezer Crafts in 1771. It is said that the first innkeeper stored arms in the inn as the Revolution became imminent, and that Minutemen took a drop of refreshment there before marching off to Lexington and Concord. Even though in the good Colonel's time Sturbridge held too firmly to the Puritan tradition to observe Christmas, The Publick House today celebrates with strolling minstrels, scarlet-clad yeomen, wenches, a jester, and a sprite who rides in on the yule log and hangs the mistletoe. As the minstrel strums his dulcimer and the rafters ring with the merry songs of Christmas, guests gather by an open fire in the taproom where Lafayette and his son stopped to rest in 1824. Then they follow the Boar's Head procession upstairs for the feast. The menu would cheer the heart of any Englishman—roast beef, roast suckling pig, glazed turkeys and hams, stuffed goose, molded salads, plum pudding, and Christmas pies.

*S*trong hands to weak,
old hands to young,
Around the Christmas board,
touch hands.
—William H. H. Murray, 1840–1904

Mrs. Julia Cook's blue eyes grow
even warmer as she recalls Christ-

mas at her childhood home in Green-field, Massachusetts, half a century ago. "It was a time when the whole family came home—everyone who was away at school or working in another town —they all came for Christmas. The ones who traveled the farthest usually sent their gifts home ahead—and there was such excitement when packages were delivered to the door! Our house seemed to be the gathering place for the boys and girls in the neighbor-hood, and they'd all come over to help us trim our tree on Christmas Eve. Then we'd go ice skating on the pond in back of the house; and when we came in, Mother would have hot chocolate and cake for us. . . ."

Under the gaslights of Louisburg Square, all of Boston comes home on Christmas Eve, returning in spirit to a simpler day. The red brick Federalist town houses on Beacon Hill, with their bow windows, black shutters, and wrought-iron balconies, border cobblestone streets surrounding a central park. At dusk, the elegant draperies and inside shutters—usually closed at this hour—are pulled back, and windows pour out their golden light. Candles glow, fires blaze on hearths, and gifts sit waiting under Christmas trees. In the warm pools of light that spill outside, the young, old, rich, poor, black, white from every corner of the great old city begin to gather. One group moves closer to the doorstep of No. 11 where the bellringers will appear, and a slim boy in a knit watch cap pulls a pitch pipe from his pocket and sounds a note. Suddenly the bitter cold night is filled with "The First Noël," a soprano singing the obbligato in a clear voice. Fathers boost toddlers to their shoulders for a better view; mothers hold on to little, mittened hands. Down Pinckney Street comes a Beacon Hill resident, Miss Katharine Lyford, stepping along in her sensible shoes as spryly as those half a century younger. She is shepherding her family-for-the-night, a dozen young South American students. Pretty nuns in brown habits hurry to the window of No. 9, and upstairs a matriarch in a long red gown and a Queen Mary hat peers down at the musicians. Promptly

at 7:15 the door swings open and a gentleman in a black greatcoat and fur hat ushers out a group of matrons. They raise their Swiss bells, he gives a cue, and even the tone of the bells is silver as the carols ring out. A hush falls on the crowd as the last note dies away. Farther down the square, a young group begins to sing intricate baroque melodies. When the tune is familiar,

everyone joins in; from across the park, a boy on a trombone, a girl with an ancient cornet, and another young man with a fiddle take up the song. Soon everyone is walking again, peering down into windows at sidewalk level, stretching to see into those on the floor above. The wind blows stronger, and fingers and toes turn numb with cold. At last Miss Lyford leads her guests back up the steep, narrow, little street, past the house where Katherine Cornell lived, stopping to peek down candlelit steps to the home where the Alcott family once resided. Then Miss Lyford unlocks the door to her own unpretentious second-floor apartment and welcomes her "family" in. Sherry is poured, and fruitcake is served on rose and green heirloom plates, which are always reserved for Christmas. The songs of carolers drift up through the windows, and the hostess raises her wine glass to these young friends, no longer strangers in this foreign land. "A merry Christmas, everyone!" Her guests stand quickly and toast her in return— *Feliz Navidad!* Christmas candles sparkle in their eyes, and they, too, are "home" for Christmas.

The clock chimes; it is time to leave for the candlelight service at King's Chapel. The chancel is banked with poinsettias, and the scent of pine is

like frankincense in this beautiful church which has celebrated the Christ Child's birth for more than two hundred years. To the accompaniment of a harpsichord, a recorder, and a thrilling counterpoint of twentieth-century sounds, the King's Chapel choir sings. And suddenly hearts sing, and hands clasp hands—and here, and all over New England and the waiting world, it is truly Christmas!

"And I *do* come home at Christmas. We all do, or we all should. We all come home, or ought to come home, for a short holiday—the longer, the better—from the great boarding-school, where we are forever working at our arithmetical slates, to take, and give a rest."

—Charles Dickens, *A Christmas Tree*